Predict It!

Dona Herweck Rice

Consultant

Michelle Alfonsi
Engineer, Southern California
Aerospace Industry

Image Credits: Cover & p.1 Hero Images Inc./Alamy; p.14 (bottom) Arctic Images/Alamy; p.14 (top left) blickwinkel/Alamy; pp.2–3 Hero Images Inc./Alamy; pp.26–27 The LIFE Picture Collection/Getty Images/Isis Sousa/Margaret Sarah Carpenter/National Endowment for the Arts; pp.8 (bottom left), 14 (top right) iStock; pp.28–29 (illustrations) Janelle Bell-Martin; p.24 U.S. Civilian/NASA; p.19 Photostock Israel/Science Photo Library; p.5 (right) AIP Emilio Segré Visual/Science Source; p.5 (left) Mike Agliolo/Science Source; p.22 USGS; all other images from Shutterstock.

Library of Congress Cataloging-in-Publication Data

Rice, Dona, author.
Predict it! / Dona Herweck Rice.
pages cm
Summary: "How do we know anything about anything? Because someone got curious and asked a question! Scientists use experiments to test their predictions. Making predictions is an important scientific practice. Ask questions, make predictions, and test possible answers to see what you discover next!"— Provided by publisher.
Audience: K to grade 3.
Includes index.
ISBN 978-1-4807-4652-7 (pbk.)
ISBN 978-1-4807-5096-8 (ebook)
1. Science—Methodology—Juvenile literature.
2. Forecasting—Juvenile literature. I. Title.
Q175.2.R525 2015
507.2'1—dc23
2014034283

Teacher Created Materials
5301 Oceanus Drive
Huntington Beach, CA 92649-1030
http://www.tcmpub.com
ISBN 978-1-4807-4652-7

Printed by: 51497
Printed in: Taiwan

Table of Contents

Tricky Business

"**Prediction** is very difficult, especially if it's about the future."

That was said by famous scientist (and comic) Niels Bohr. Okay, okay, he wasn't a comic. But what he said is pretty funny, right? And Bohr knew what he was talking about! As a scientist, he knew about **evidence** and making predictions. He also knew about testing predictions. Again and again and again and again and . . .

Working Together

Niels Bohr is famous for winning a Nobel Prize in science for his work with atoms. But he's also famous for telling all scientists and nations that the work of science should be shared openly and freely.

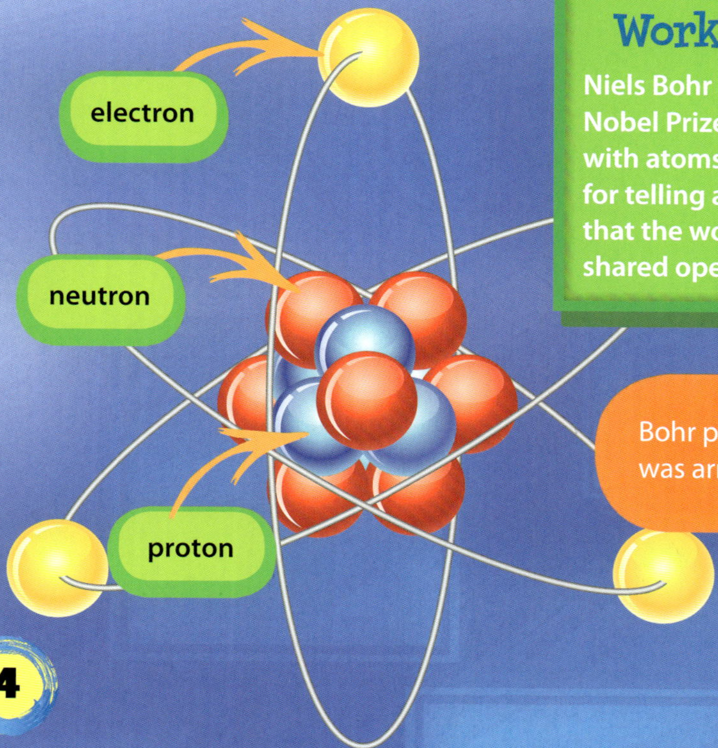

Bohr predicted that the atom was arranged in this way.

It's tricky business! Making scientific predictions isn't the easiest work out there. But it's worth it. If you are someone who likes to solve puzzles or mysteries, the world of science is a good place for you. There's no limit to what you can think, explore, and do.

In fact, I predict that you will be a very good scientist!

Niels Bohr

You can't really hold an atom in your hands. But your hands are made of atoms. Who could predict that?

Scientific Method

There's a method to their madness! The **scientific method**, that is.

Every good piece of science begins with the scientific method. What exactly is the scientific method, you ask? Well, I'm happy to tell you! But listen up, because I'm only going to say it once! (Of course, you can always read it again and again, but that's a different matter.)

Are you listening?

Are you sure?

And a One, and a Two . . .

Here's the scientific method, in six easy steps:

- observation and **research**
- **hypothesis**
- prediction
- experimentation
- **analysis**
- report

Is the hypothesis true? Great! Report your results. Not true? Report your results anyway, make a new hypothesis, and try again!

Note: Scientists don't always do the steps of the scientific method in the same order. . . and they may even repeat some steps!

Okay, here it is. The scientific method is a plan used to investigate a question in science. In other words, it's the method for "doing" science well. Get it?

After all, why do something if you're not going to do it right? The scientific method is doing science right.

Good science work must be planned. It starts with an idea, something that the scientist is curious about. Maybe, "Hey, why can't I get that song out of my head?" Or, "I wonder why my lawn turned brown even though I watered it?"

The scientist thinks about the idea. Then he or she **observes** and does research to learn what is already known about it. For example, the scientist sees her dog lift its leg on the lawn every day. "Hmmm," she thinks. "I wonder what that means?" She might research whether other dogs do the same thing when they visit the lawn.

From that, the scientist forms a hypothesis. A hypothesis is something the scientist assumes from what she already knows. It's based on information that has been gathered. Maybe it's "Canine urine* kills a lawn."

*That's right, dog pee.

True or False?

What makes a hypothesis testable? It must be something that can be proven true or false. You can test the idea that all yo-yos are red by looking at every yo-yo in the world. You just need to find one yo-yo that's a different color to know the hypothesis is false. But even if you couldn't look at every yo-yo in the world, this is still a testable hypothesis. You just haven't proven it true yet.

What comes next takes super-science brainpower! The scientist needs to test the hypothesis. And so, she makes a prediction. Take the lawn, for example.

The Right Hypothesis

Keep in mind three important things when forming a hypothesis:

- It should be something that's not already known.
- It's a statement, not a question.
- It must be testable.

Test It!

Next in the scientific method, the scientist does an **experiment**. Experiments are tests. The tests check the hypothesis. Scientists need to check off every possibility. And they have to get the same results every time. If they don't, they haven't proven the hypothesis.

After the experiments, the scientist studies the results to see what they mean. This is called *analysis*. Do the results prove the hypothesis? Disprove it? The scientist either rejects or accepts the hypothesis.

Fact or Fiction

Many people use the word *theory* to describe an untested idea about why something happens. It might correctly describe why something happens. Or it might be wildly inaccurate. We don't know because the idea hasn't been tested and proven factual.

Scientists use the word *theory* to describe an explanation (supported by the scientific method) about why something happens. Scientific theories are only formed after making many observations and testing a hypothesis many times.

In the past, people thought fairy mischief caused their cows' milk to sour.

Finally, a good scientist shares the results. He or she reports what was done and what was found. Then, other scientists test it, too. And if *they* prove it, they have a big science party. Well, maybe they don't have a party—but they should!

And that, my friends, is the scientific method!

The word *experiment* comes from an old word that means "try."

Now, How About Prediction?

Each step of the scientific method is important. And prediction is just as important as the other steps.

You know now that a scientist must research first. Next comes the hypothesis. Then, with all that good information in mind, the scientist predicts. But think about this: The prediction isn't just any old guess. It's based on what is already known. It's an *educated* guess. It's not a guess pulled from thin air. It's not a guess that just sounds cool or the scientist hopes will be true. There is good reason for that guess to be made. And there's good reason that it may be proven true.

"Using a crystal ball works great," said *no* scientist ever! It's science, not imagination.

This or That!

Making a prediction isn't just about guessing what will happen in the future. It's about deciding what you think will happen if you do one thing instead of the other.

- I predict that eating candy for breakfast, lunch, and dinner will give me a stomachache.
- I predict that if I feed my plant soda, it will die.
- I predict a slug will change direction if I stand in front of it.

These are all predictions! They are educated guesses based on what you think will happen.

One way to make a prediction is to think about what would happen if your hypothesis were true and what would happen if it were not true.

biology

botany

In the Lab

Some companies, colleges, and even countries run laboratories, or labs, where science research is done year-round. No matter the problem or question, there is probably a lab somewhere studying it.

geology

This is why reporting scientific results is so important. Every scientist working on a hypothesis doesn't work from scratch. Other scientists have already done and reported a lot of work. The scientist can study other scientists' work. So when he or she makes a prediction, there's already a lot of good science to back it up. The scientist learns as much as possible about the topic. Then, the prediction is a smart one.

Remember Niels Bohr? This is why he wanted every scientist to share research freely. He thought the advancement of science was more important than the advancement of a single scientist. It's like, "Hey, we're all in this together. Let's help one another out."

Things sure are a lot easier that way!

Patient Predictions

It can take a long time to have a hypothesis accepted as true. Some experiments have been going for over 50 years. It can take that long to watch your test subjects. Other times, scientists can't test their ideas until new technology has been developed.

Be Specific

A hypothesis is a general statement. It's a "big idea." It says how you think the science topic works. But a prediction is **specific**. It narrows the hypothesis in a way that can be tested. It is used to show if the hypothesis is true. You experiment to test your prediction. And the tests are specific, too.

One way to get specific is to think about cause and effect. In cause and effect, we see that one thing leads to another thing. So, we can test a prediction and see that every time we do step A, step B happens. But here's the thing. We don't know if A is the cause of B. We know they are related in some way, but we can't assume that A caused B. (We might think we know, because it sure seems like it. But we don't really know until we can prove it.) We have to get rid of every factor that could be the cause in order to show the direct cause and effect between A and B.

From Hypothesis to Prediction

A hypothesis is an explanation for why something happens. So you might hypothesize that "kids have a better sense of humor than adults." A prediction is used to show that a hypothesis is true or false.

So, your prediction might be "more of my classmates than teachers will laugh at my joke about the chicken crossing the road."

Then, you'll run an experiment in which you tell the same joke to your classmates and teachers and count the number of laughs you get.

And here's another important thing to know. When you experiment, your goal is *to try to prove your hypothesis wrong!* That's right! You have to try everything you can to shoot it down. It's only after you try all the ways to prove it wrong and it still holds up that you know the hypothesis is true.

Take Control

Of course, all of this can be hard to keep straight. That's why scientists use something called a **control group**. A control group is something that is used as a standard for comparison. It isn't affected by the thing being tested.

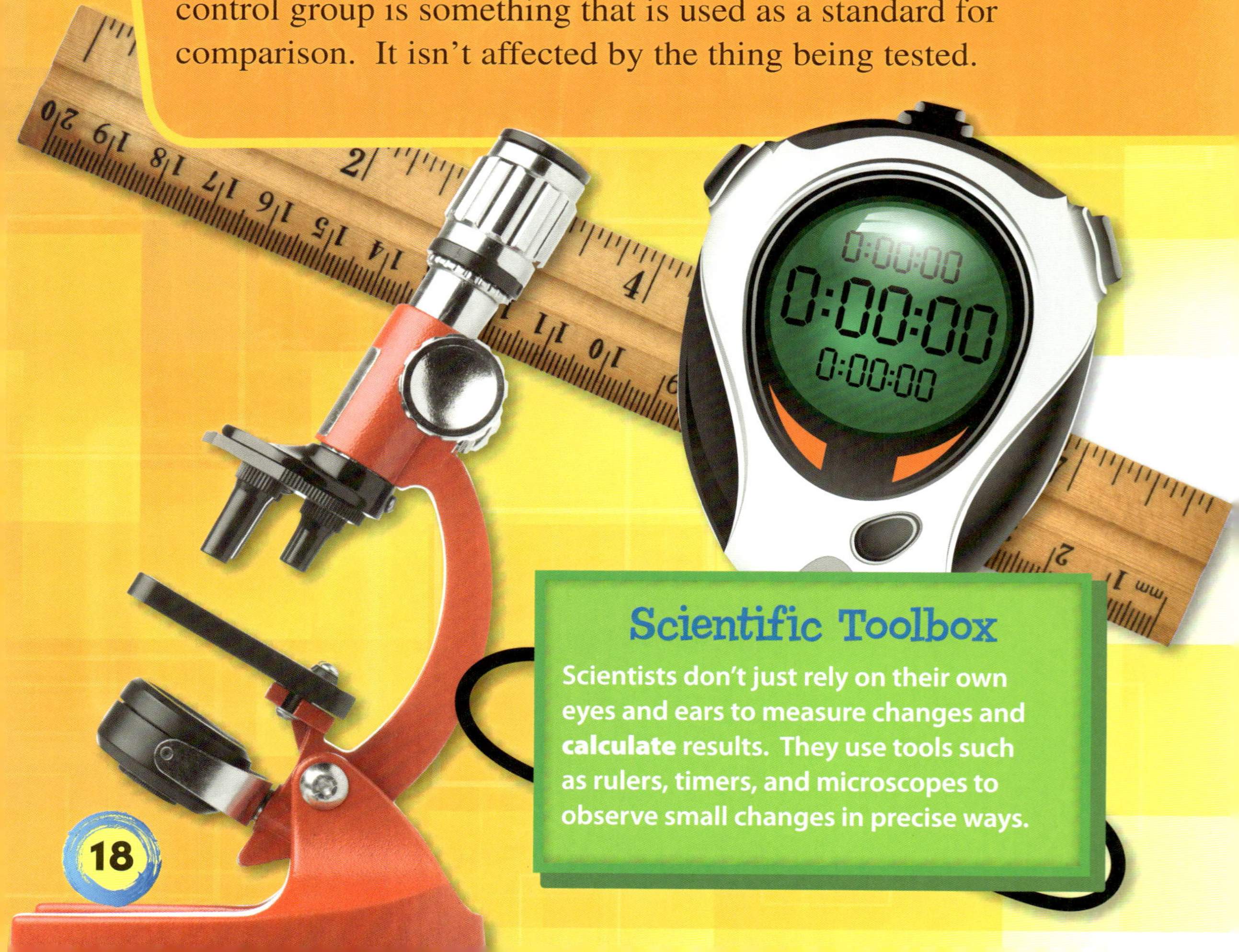

Scientific Toolbox

Scientists don't just rely on their own eyes and ears to measure changes and **calculate** results. They use tools such as rulers, timers, and microscopes to observe small changes in precise ways.

Okay, what does *that* mean? Here's an example. Let's say that you want to find the best fertilizer for a kind of plant. You can experiment to find the best fertilizer to use. So you do everything to the control plant that you do to other plants (like water it and give it sunlight), *except* you don't give the plant that fertilizer.

Using the control group helps you narrow down cause and effect. It helps you be specific. And being specific helps you get your answer!

	control plant	test plant
week 1	1.0 cm	1.0 cm
week 2	1.5 cm	1.6 cm
week 3	1.65 cm	1.75 cm
week 4	1.70 cm	2.0 cm

measuring a flower grown without fertilizer

measuring a flower grown with fertilizer

It's Probable

Another way to make a prediction is to use **probability**. Scientists study patterns. They learn the pattern, and in time, they can make really good guesses about what will happen based on the pattern. Then later, they can decide how likely it is that something else will happen.

Try this. Flip a coin. It will land heads up or tails up. Flip it again. It will land heads up or tails up again. Do it again, and the same thing happens. Each time you flip, it has an equal chance of being heads up as it does of being tails up. If you flip it a bunch of times, about half the time it will come up heads and the other half will be tails. Probability shows us that it's very unlikely for the coin to always be heads or even to mostly be heads. If you run the test enough, it's always half and half. And it almost never lands on its edge!

Scientists know how probability works. When they see and study a pattern, they can use that pattern to make future predictions. It's not luck. It's science.

The Mathematics of Prediction

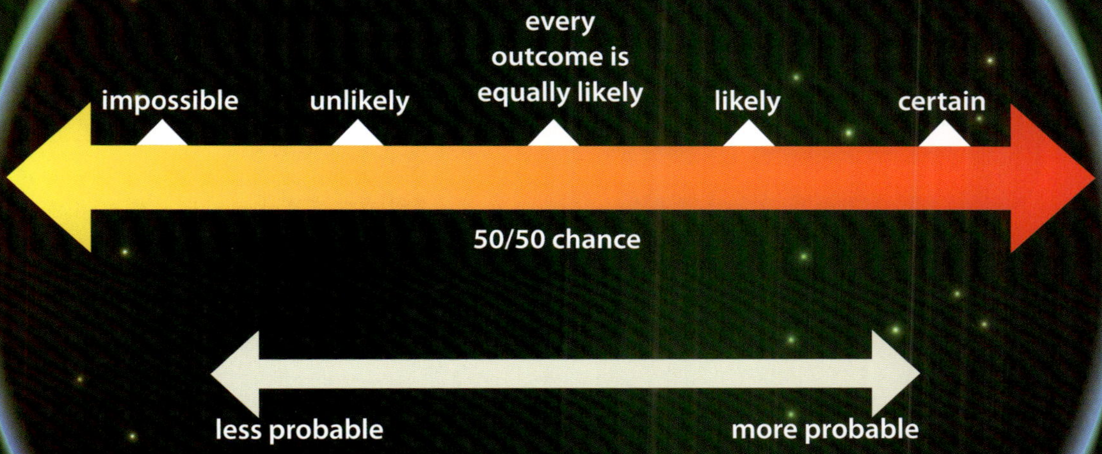

Math is very useful in making predictions. For example, scientists use math to predict events such as a lunar eclipse. They use the time of the event in the past to calculate and predict the time of the event in the future.

Scientists use probability to help predict earthquakes. No one knows when an earthquake will strike. At least, no one knows yet! But we can make good predictions based on patterns.

California has a lot of earthquakes. Most of them are small, but some are pretty big. Many happen along the San Andreas Fault. Scientists look at the evidence. They study Earth to see when and where earthquakes have happened along the fault in the past. They find the average time between earthquakes. They see how big the

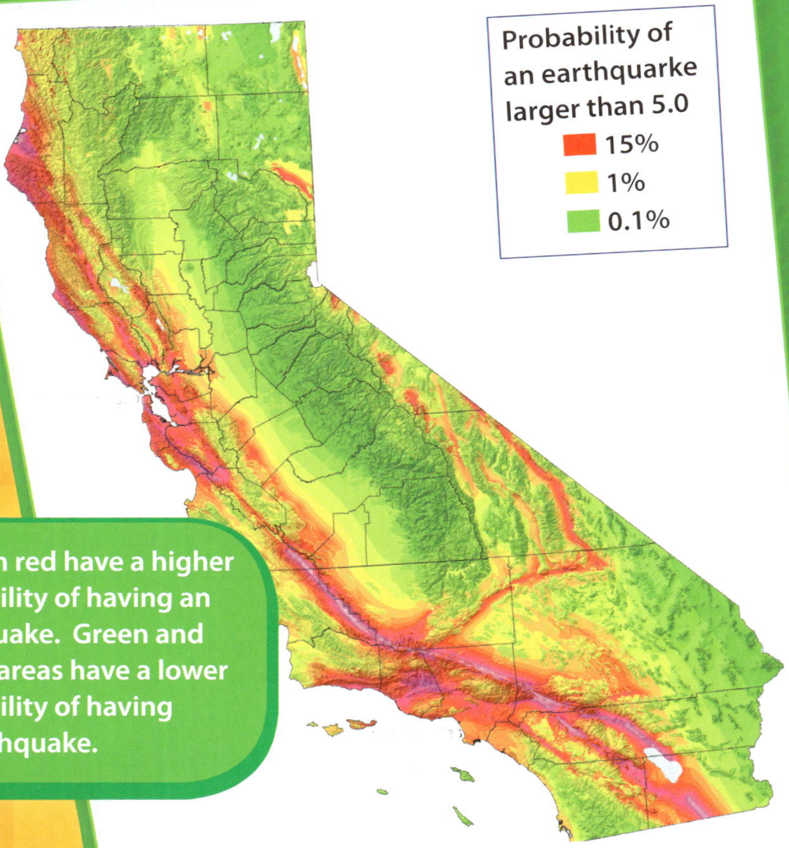

Areas in red have a higher probability of having an earthquake. Green and yellow areas have a lower probability of having an earthquake.

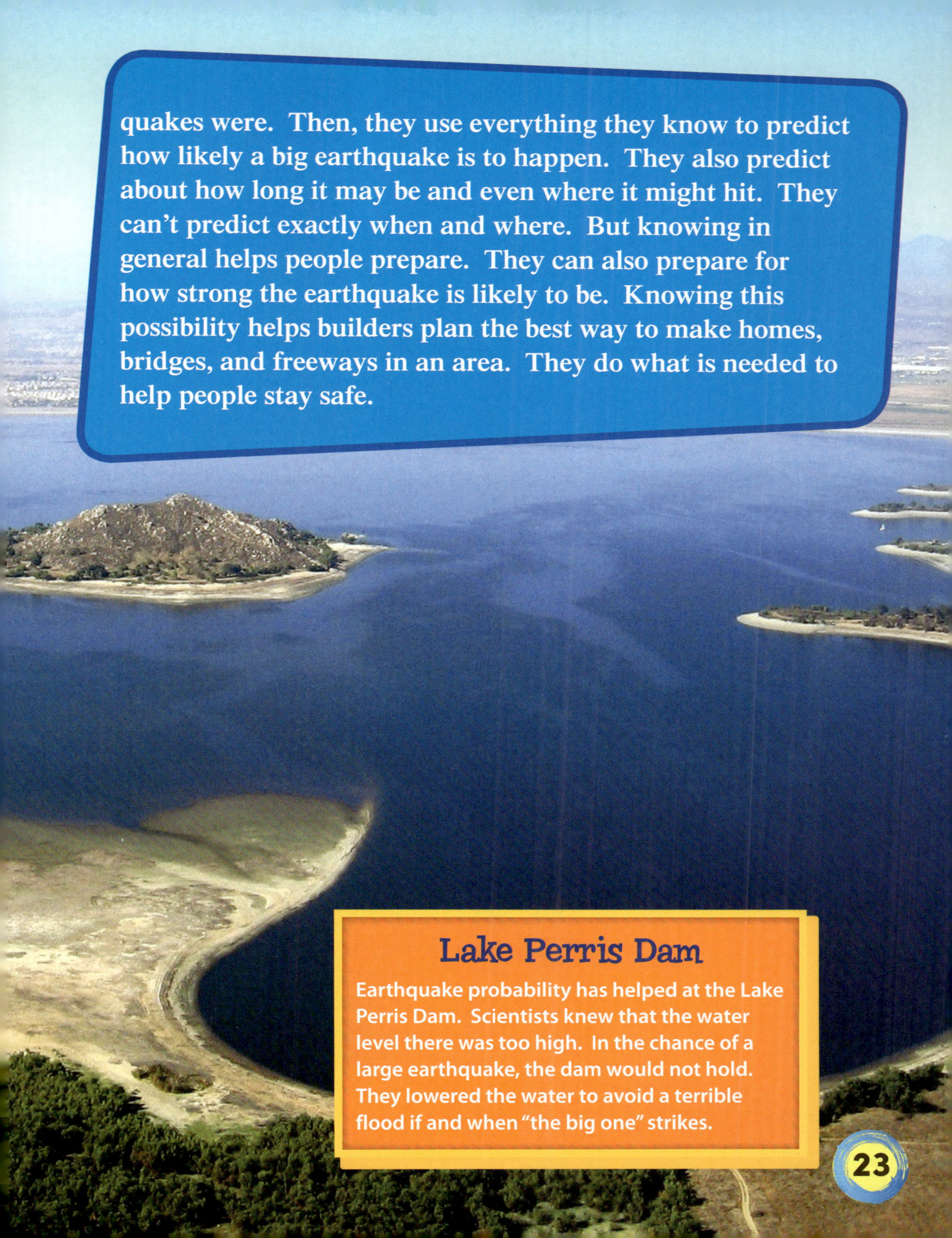

quakes were. Then, they use everything they know to predict how likely a big earthquake is to happen. They also predict about how long it may be and even where it might hit. They can't predict exactly when and where. But knowing in general helps people prepare. They can also prepare for how strong the earthquake is likely to be. Knowing this possibility helps builders plan the best way to make homes, bridges, and freeways in an area. They do what is needed to help people stay safe.

Lake Perris Dam

Earthquake probability has helped at the Lake Perris Dam. Scientists knew that the water level there was too high. In the chance of a large earthquake, the dam would not hold. They lowered the water to avoid a terrible flood if and when "the big one" strikes.

Don't Change!

Let's say you have made your prediction. Now, you are testing it. But your experiments start to show that your prediction isn't correct. You may be tempted to change your prediction. If so, STOP

Testing 1, 2, 3 . . .

Scientific questions can be big and meaty, like "What is time?" or precise, like "How much fuel is required to send a rocket to the moon?" Some can't be answered with just one test. Don't worry if you need to perform several experiments to answer your questions. That just means you're asking good questions!

Never change your prediction or hypothesis during any part of the scientific method. *After* you have seen it through to the end, *then* you can think about a change. But you have to stick with your hypothesis while you're testing it.

Remember, you are trying to prove your hypothesis wrong. And most of the time it *will* be proven wrong! That's the way of science.

Written in Stone

Even if a hypothesis isn't proven false right away, it might be proven false later—much later in some cases! Isaac Newton was the first to explain accurately how planets and other large objects move. For hundreds of years, his hypothesis was supported. But when Albert Einstein created his theory of gravity, Newton's hypothesis was proven false. Newton's work was still important. But hypotheses only last until a better one comes along.

You may be tempted to think of this as a "fail." But it's not! All it means is that the testing showed something new. You have new information to work with. The new information can be added to your research. Then, you can make a new hypothesis and a new prediction. You can start testing again.

It takes courage to admit you're wrong. But science isn't about proving your hypothesis. It's about getting to the truth. And it usually takes a lot of "not true" to get there!

So, all you scientists out there, stay focused! Make some predictions! Test them. Stay determined! Make some more predictions. And then test them some more! Follow this method, and you'll be in very good company.

Think Like a Scientist

How can you form a good scientific prediction? Experiment and find out!

What to Get

- sandwich bag
- sharpened pencils
- water

What to Do

1. Fill the sandwich bag about three-fourths full with water and seal it.

2. Using the hypothesis *Water will leak through a hole*, predict if water will leak from the bag when you poke pencils through it.

3. Have a friend hold the bag while you poke a pencil straight through one side and out the other. Don't remove the pencil. Repeat with a second and third pencil. What happened? Was your prediction correct?

Note: Plastic bags are made of a material that stretches when you poke the bag. The material "grabs" around the pencil and forms a seal. Water shouldn't leak through the holes.

Glossary

analysis—study of something to learn about its parts, what it does, and how it relates to other things

calculate—to find a number or answer by using math

control group—the group in an experiment that is not changed like the other groups

evidence—something that shows that something else exists or is true

experiment—a scientific test performed to learn about something

hypothesis—an idea that is not proven and needs to be studied further

observes—watches and studies closely

prediction—an educated guess based on the information you know

probability—the chance that something will happen

research—to carefully study something

scientific method—steps used by scientists to test ideas through experiments and observation

specific—clear and exact

Index

Your Turn!

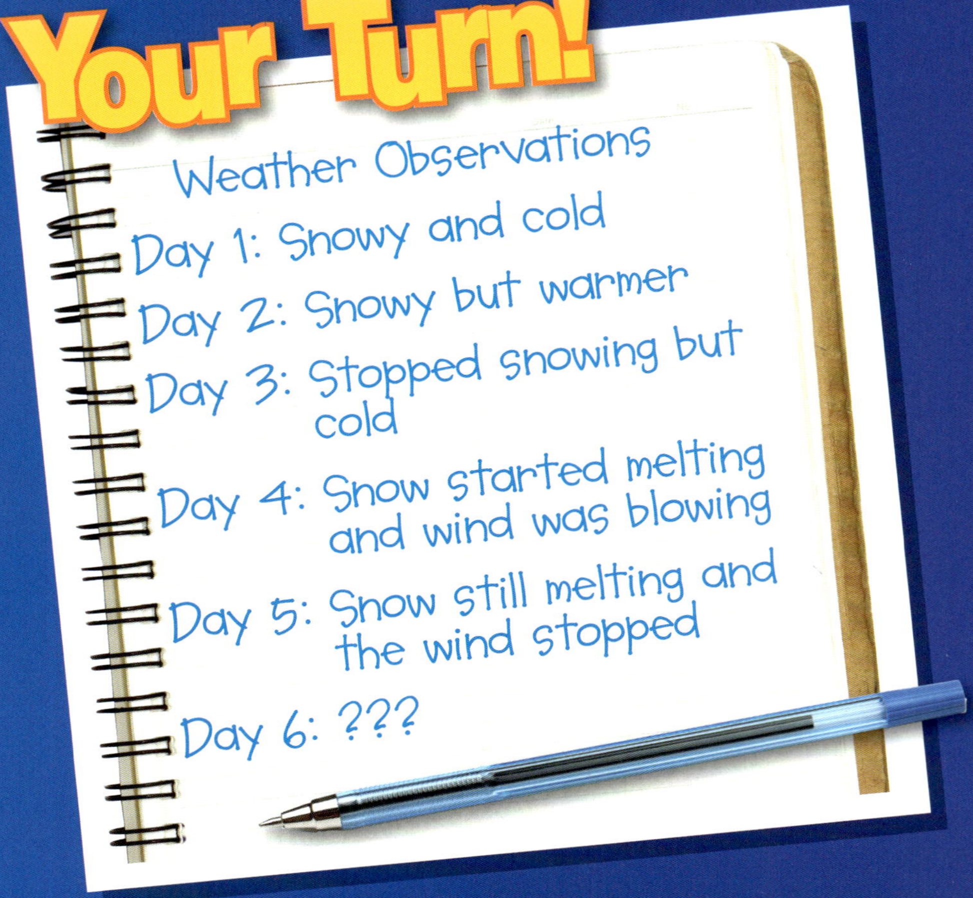

Weather Forecast

Pay attention to the weather for five days. Record the temperature and weather conditions each day. Based on your observations, make a prediction about what the weather will be like on the sixth day. On the sixth day, determine if you were correct!